Dedicated to Rob
Smith and Terry Darmondy
who both love the Guitar.

The Guitar

Wood or plastic
An instrument of
Wonder, awe and
Excitement.

When it is struck
The right way
It produces a
Melody,precise
And with Rhythm

And Sway.

It has brought
Much Delight to
Many a person
In the hands of
A young man
Or Woman
It is a symbol
Of rebellion,angst
Or Violence with
Music .

The Guitar wood
Or Plastic, simple
In construction,
Simple in construction.
Used in the USA
Or the Backstreet's
Of Africa?
The impact is there
The Same.
A thing of beauty,
Angst, wonder
And Delight.
In Praise of
The Guitar... John C Burt

Sing the Blues
On My Old Guitar.

The Blues,
Twelve Bars Blues
On my Old, Banged
Up and Missing
A String Guitar.

The Blues A Music
Of Pain and Loss
And coming out
Of oppression,Pain
And Violence ....

Blues, Full of
Rthym, Sway
Melodic and
Simply Blue
And Full of the
Blues.....
Of Life and
Circumstances .

Sing Me the Blues
On My Old Guitar
Banging Away on
The strings of
The Old Guitar ..

Searing Pain
And Loss Coming
Through the Melodic
Rthym of the Blues ...

Sometimes the Blues
Becomes Rock and Roll
With Melodic Harmony .
Yet Me and My
Old Guitar Will
Always Sing the Pain,
Angst and Loss
And Grief of
The Blues ......

Sing Me The Blues
On My Old Guitar
Missing a String
With A Few Dinks,
Chips of Paint Missing
Yet it Still sings the
Blues.........

John C Burt

Punk, The Blues With Political Pain ...

Punk Music the pain, Violence and Angst of The Anti - Establishment Movement .. Coming out of All Places Thatcher's United Kingdom ...

Music with Violence Put it up too Loud

And It will do
Violence to Your
Ears.

Punk Music the Music
Of A Lost Generation,
De-enfranchised By
The powerful Elite
Of the Society,
Economically,
Socially,
And Politically .

The Pain of A
Generation ....
Of Young Men and
Women...
Would they be forever
Lost? Where would
They find Redemption
For their Souls ?

Punk Music offered
Redemption But At
A Cost .....

Listening to Punk Music

You Were An Outcast And One Who Had Not Bought Into The Establishment Dream of A White Picket Fence, And A Brick House with Rose Bushes in Front Of it …………

Punk Music Thought Rebellion,Pain and Angst and Violence with Lyrics

Was The Answer
But In the End
It was Not the
Messiah or the
Redemptive Factor
It Promised.
Punk Music the
Blues With Political
Pain.

Heartbeat of
A Nation .....

John C Burt

Lullaby By Guitar ..

O Guitar of Mine
Sing Me A Lullaby
Make it Soft And
Gentle And Slow ..
Send Me to Sleep.
Send Me to Sleep.

Hitting each String
In Unison, with
Melodic Rthym.
Much Like the

Rocking and Swaying
Of the Trees in
The Wind....
Let the Wind blow
Through the Strings
Of my Old Guitar...
It Has Seen Better
Days and Yet
It Can Still Produce
A Lullaby .....

Rock Me to Sleep
Melodic strumming
Of the Strings......

Banging, Plucking
And Stroking ....
My Old Guitar
To Produce A
Rhythmic Melodic Lullaby.
Sleep to the Music
As the Rthym takes
Over, The Rthym Of
Sleep and Dreams
And the Endless
Vapors of A Long
Dark Night of
Slumber .....

The Twang of the
High Note the
Top E string, Screaming
Out its Constant Melody
And Rthym ....
Beckoning the Hearer
To the Sleep of the
Endless Variety.
Lullaby By Guitar
Lullaby By Guitar
Using the top 'E' string
In Precise Rthym And
Strumming ....
John C Burt

Old Rock And Roll

Rock Music the Heavy Kind
Play it Loud, Hard And With
Strength And Sometimes Showing
Violence And Pain .
But always a High Volume,
The Pain And Violence
Cannot Help But Come Through.

They Say Punk Music Was
The Music of The Generation
But Give The Old Rock And Roll
At High Volume At Anytime ......
Old Rock And Roll One With
A Heavy Bass Beat of the Drums
Pulsating And Banging And
Pounding the Rhythm of The
Generations ....

Rock And Roll
Anti - Establishment
Anti - Politics
Anti - Authority
The Music of The
Generations .....

Screaming Guitar Solo's
Pulsate Rock And Roll
Melodies. Like Birds Screaming
In Flight When Coming For Their
Prey.

Lead Guitar Solo's Screaming Out
In Pain, Angst ....
With Occasional Violence
Being Done to the Brain And
Ears of the Hearer ....
Old Rock And Roll
May It Never Die.....
The Music of the Generations ...
John C Burt

The African Guitar.

Tin Can With Some
Strings   .
Best Quality Guitar On
The Planet.
Used and Played By
Street Musicians
On the Streets Throughout
The African Continent.

Played Loud, Hard
And With Melodic Rthym.

Accompanied By The
Drums, Any Form of
Drum   ...
Made Out of Iron And
Steel.
The Banging And Crashing
Of the Drums Accompanies
The African Guitar of
The African Streets ....

It Is A Wonder To Behold..
Played Expertly By A
Musical Artist .

It Can Be Full Of
Pain, Sorrow And
Loss   ....
Or It Can Be Happy
And Joyful Sounds
Produced ....
Bringing The Joy And
Laughter of The African
Streets To Life In Musical
Form ....

For One Who has Little
The African Guitar

Offers An Outlet In
The Form of Music .
The Music of The
African Streets.
The Music of The
African Streets.
The African Guitar ...

John C Burt

The Passion And Pain
Of My Old Guitar ..

The Passion And Pain
Of My Old Guitar.
It Can Evoke The Heights
Of Both Passion And Pain
In Unending Quantities...
The Searing Passion
And Pain of Loss And
Grief .
The Searing Passion
And Pain of Ecstasy And

Love And Romance ..
The Passion And Pain
Of My Old Guitar ...

Passion And Pain
Go Together, Inseparable
And We cannot Live
Without Having Both.
The Passion And Pain
Of My Old Guitar ..

John C Burt

The Guitarist Named Terry.

There Was A Guitarist
Named Terry.
Terry Loved Playing The
Guitar.
He Could Produce Amazing
Sounds On His Old
Guitar.

Terry Loved Singing Old
Blues Harmony Gospel Songs
From Ages Past And
Getting Others to Sing And
Rejoice In Them .

Give Me The Old Time Gospel
Songs of A Bygone Day.
With The Blues Running

Through Their Views
And Verses.
The Good Old Gospel Songs
Of A Bygone Era.

Terry was An Artist
With His Old Guitars ..
He could Play Any Form
Of Music On His Old Guitars .
The Guitar In His Hands
Literally Sang As He Strummed
Its Strings ....

The Heights Of Ecstasy, Pain
Passion and The Blues were His
Vocation....... He Did This With
Unending Rthym And Blues In Every
Form And Song ......

The Walls Of The Rooms
He Was Playing In Literally
Swayed and bucked in
Rthym With the Beat of the
Strumming of His Old Guitar.

The Guitarist Named Terry ...

John C Burt

Rob And The Music
Of The Beatles ...

There Is A Man Called
Rob who Plays Guitar
And Sings In A Beatles
Cover Band ...
Rob Loves The Music
And Passion Of The
Beatles So Much That
He Plays Them In the
Club-land of Sydney.

The Beatles The Voice
Of A Generation
Constant And Dynamic
The Music of A Bygone
Era .
Teenage Rebellion And
Angst and Pain And
Passion .
All on Show at Once So
Haircuts To Be Like
Them   ....

Beatlemania Is Alive
And Well In The Club-
land
Of Sydney ....

The Music Of A Bygone
Generation And Era.
It Still Pulsates As Rob
Sings It And Plays Guitar
Producing The Sounds
In Time With The Rthym
Of the Music of The
Beatles.

The Voices of The Past,
Echo Through The Club-
land Of Sydney.
Bringing Security And
Warmth Of A Bygone Era
Of Teenage Angst, Pain,
Passion
And Even Rebellion ....
Rob And The Music Of The
Beatles Is Alive And
Well in The Club-land Of
Sydney .....
John C Burt

The Confessions Of A Frustrated Guitarist.

I Believe That Inside Of Each Of Us Is A Frustrated Guitarist...
Frustrated Because We Cannot Read Music And Understand The Notes And Instead Just Play Some Chords We May know

From Our Faded Memories
Of Our Past Excursions
Into The Land Of the
Guitar And Its Music
And Forms .....

I Am A Frustrated Guitarist,
I Would Love to Be A
Master Guitarist. But
Finding The Time To
Pursue The Passion And
Pain Of the Study Of The
Music of the Guitarist

Is Sometimes Too Hard?

Which Is Why We Are
Talking About The
Confessions of A
Frustrated Guitarist ?

The Chords I Play
Never Seem To have a
Rthym or Rhyme?
But Are Instead haphazard
And Come From My
Banging and Consoling

Of the Strings Of My Guitar .....
I am Trying to bring Some Sense to The Music Coming Out Of My Soul? My Own Music,Played My Way, With My Tired Old Voice.....
I bang away, plucking And Caressing the Strings Seeking To Make A Sound That Makes Some Sense?

The Confessions Of A Frustrated Guitarist... Long May We Play !

John C Burt

Lightning Source UK Ltd.
Milton Keynes UK
UKRC020307120619
344091UK00007B/46